SAY HELLO WHEREVER YOU GO

MUSIC STRATEGIES, SONGS AND ACTIVITIES FOR GRADES K-2

BY JOHN JACOBSON AND JANET DAY

LESSON PLANS BY CHARYL GRANATELLA, JUDY HERRINGTON AND CONNIE SCHMIDT, LINDA RANN AND ELLEN SHULER

TABLE OF CONTENTS

The complete National Arts Standards and additional materials relating to the Standards are available from MENC: **www.menc.org**.

HAL•LEONARD® CORPORATION

7777 W. BLUEMOUND RD. P.O. BOX 13819 MILWAUKEE, WI 53213

Visit Hal Leonard Online at
www.halleonard.com

INTRODUCTION

It is true! What you learn through music, you never forget! Think about these timeless learning songs:

- The Alphabet Song (letters)
- Fifty Nifty United States (names of the states)
- The Ants Go Marching In (counting)
- Ten in the Bed (counting backwards)
- Head and Shoulders (parts of the body)
- John Jacob Jingleheimer Schmidt (dynamics, volume)

and the list goes on and on!

This song collection, designed for the younger grades, takes this concept of learning through music and expands the topic base. These songs will teach your students:

- Types of dinosaurs
- How to count money
- Rhyming words
- Spelling
- Names of the planets
- How to tell time
- High sounds verses low sounds
- Healthy habits
- Rules for safety

and SO much more.

Coordinate with the primary classroom teachers to reinforce with music what they are learning in the classroom. For example, when students are studying dinosaurs, keep the learning going with "The Dinosaur Walk." Not only will they learn the names and characteristics of several dinosaur types, but they will also learn steady beat and verse/chorus (AB) form. Are the students learning how to tell time in their classrooms? Reinforce this concept in the music room with "What Time Is It, Mr. Clock?" Use their "human" hands to create the time on your kid-size clock and they will never forget how to tell time.

When you create an atmosphere of fun, adventure and creativity, the music and learning comes naturally. We hope this collection brings you many class periods of rewarding lessons for hundreds of young learners that enjoy music class!

John Jacobson and Janet Day

HELLO

ABOUT THE WRITERS

John Jacobson

In October of 2001 President George Bush named John Jacobson a Point of Light award winner for his "dedication to providing young people involved in the arts opportunities to combine music, charitable giving and community service." John is the founder and volunteer president of America Sings! Inc., a non-profit organization that encourages young performers to use their time and talents for community service.

With a bachelor's degree in Music Education from the University of Wisconsin-Madison and a Master's Degree in Liberal Studies from Georgetown University, John is recognized internationally as a creative and motivating speaker for teachers and students involved in choral music education. He is the author and composer of many musicals and choral works that have been performed by millions of children worldwide, as well as educational videos and tapes that have helped music educators excel in their individual teaching arenas, all published exclusively by Hal Leonard Corporation.

John has staged hundreds of huge music festival ensembles in his association with Walt Disney Productions and directed productions featuring thousands of young singers including NBC's national broadcast of the Macy's Thanksgiving Day Parade, presidential inaugurations and more. John stars in children's musical and exercise videotapes, most recently the series Jjump! A Fitness Program for Children and is the Senior Contributing Writer for John Jacobson's Music Express, an educational magazine for young children.

Janet Klevberg Day is editor-in-chief of *Music Express Magazine* and a choral editor for Hal Leonard Corporation. She received her B.S. degree in instrumental and choral music from Mayville State University in Mayville, ND and her M.M. degree with a choral emphasis from Arizona State University. She has taught at the elementary and junior high levels in Grand Forks, ND and has several choral arrangements and elementary resources published through Hal Leonard Corporation. She lives in Elm Grove, WI with her husband and two sons.

ADD AND SUBTRACT. THAT'S A FACT!

Lesson Plan by Judy Herrington and Connie Schmidt

LEARNING THROUGH
music

This lively song will give you and your students the opportunities to create fun learning experiences in your classroom. Through this song, your students can explore mathematical facts and patterns as well as music skills. It will be especially helpful and meaningful when you adapt it to your needs, making it "fit your classroom."

LESSON GOALS

* Sing in tune
* Maintain steady beat while singing
* Practice math facts
* Recognize and practice patterns (number, rhythmic and melodic)
* Develop increased understanding of note value equivalencies
* Have fun working and learning together

This lesson addresses National Standards for Arts Education, Music Grades K-4: 1e, 2b, 6a.

MATERIALS

* CD track 1 (with vocals); track 20 (accompaniment)
* CD player
* Percussion instruments
* Flash cards of math facts
* Number Chart (10 columns across; write in the numbers 1 – 10 in first row; 11 – 20 in second row; 21-30 in third row; and so on)

START

Explain to the students that the song has two distinct parts: the "add and subtract" melody (A section) and the "math fact" (B section). Once the two sections are learned, they can alternate.

Teaching Process for "add and subtract" A section:

1. Establish a steady beat (patschen).
2. Teacher speaks and students echo (one or two-measure phrases).
3. Replace steady beat patschen with percussion instrument and echo-sing the melody.

Teaching Tips:

* *On the lyrics, "Just so that you know" give a slight crescendo to an accented downbeat on "you."*
* *When using speech for echoes, be sure that the vocal pitch is not too low and give plenty of 'melody' to the speaking voice.*

Teaching Process for "math fact" B section:

Follow the directions indicated in the score. You may find it helpful to adjust the direction to better meet the needs of your students or to create a variation.

1. Tap the side of forehead during the "thinking measure."
2. Have child raise hand to indicate he/she is ready to answer.
3. Group should give encouragement for both correct and incorrect answers. If an incorrect answer is given, student should be given a second chance to answer correctly or chance to ask classmates for help.

Teaching Tips:

* *Practice with the entire class answering the math questions before using individual students.*
* *Select math questions based on the level of the individual student's skill.*
* *For more advanced math problems, students may enjoy working with a partner.*

Perform the piece alternating the "add and subtract" melody with the "math quiz" section. End with the "add and subtract" melody.

EXTENDED ACTIVITIES

* Add percussion instrument (i.e. woodblock) in a steady beat or with a rhythmic pattern to the "thinking measure."
* Using a number chart, count with a steady beat, adding a clap on all even numbers. Repeat, using a different body percussion on all odd numbers. Divide the class, one half class with body percussion on the even numbers, the other half on the odd numbers.

ADD AND SUBTRACT. THAT'S A FACT!

1/20

Words and Music by JOHN JACOBSON
and JANET DAY

Copyright © 2008 by HAL LEONARD CORPORATION
International Copyright Secured   All Rights Reserved

CHOO CHOO CHA CHING!

Lesson Plan by Ellen Shuler

LEARNING THROUGH music

One of the major units studied in the primary grades is money. From learning the difference between pennies, nickels and dimes to actually counting coins, the money unit is essential curriculum. Using the song "Choo Choo Cha Ching" is a great cross-curricular lesson to help teachers reinforce what is being taught in math units. Have fun with this wonderful song!

LESSON GOALS

- Sing a song in tune
- Keep a steady beat
- Sing a syncopated rhythm
- Keep a steady beat with an instrument

This lesson addresses National Standards for Arts Education, Music Grades K-4: 1b, 1e, 2b, 2d, 5a.

MATERIALS

- CD track 2 (with vocals); track 21 (accompaniment)
- CD player
- 40 pennies
- Three empty glass or plastic jars
- Large pictures of a nickel, dime and quarter

START

1. Before listening to the song, draw on the board the syncopated pattern (eighth/quarter/ eighth quarter) to match the lyrics *Choo choo cha ching* at the end of the 3rd line. Have the students clap the rhythm while saying "choo choo cha ching" to experience the uneven, syncopated feel.

2. Listen to the entire song "Choo Choo Cha Ching." Have the children tap a steady beat while listening to the song. Have a small group clap the syncopa "Choo choo cha ching" rhythm when it occurs in the song.

DEVELOP

Put three empty glass or plastic jars on a desk or table. Decorate one with a picture of a nickel, another with a picture of a dime, another with a picture of a quarter. While the students sing or listen to the song, pour the correct amount of pennies into each jar during the spoken section. Invite the children to take turns pouring the pennies into the correct jars.

REVIEW AND PERFORM

Listen again to "Choo Choo Cha Ching." Have the students play the steady beat with rhythm shakers or other classroom instruments while listening. Remind the children of the importance of keeping a steady beat.

FOR THE OLDER GRADES

Challenge your older students to come up with different words for the spoken section. Have them try to use combinations of pennies, nickels and dimes to create their own new lyrics. Example: "Two nickels make a dime" or "Four quarters make a dollar" etc.

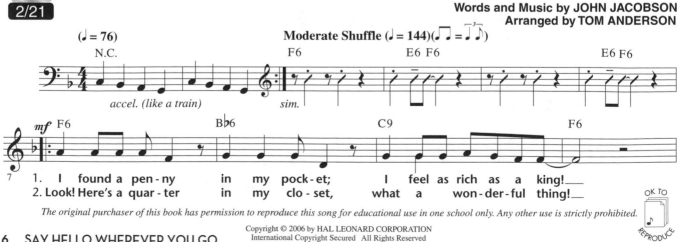

CHOO CHOO CHA CHING!

Words and Music by JOHN JACOBSON
Arranged by TOM ANDERSON

1. I found a pen-ny in my pock-et; I feel as rich as a king!
2. Look! Here's a quar-ter in my clo-set, what a won-der-ful thing!

COUNTDOWN TO CHRISTMAS

Lesson Plan by Linda Rann

LESSON GOALS

- Learn a new counting song
- Recognize a repeating rhythmic pattern
- Practice counting in a variety of ways

This lesson addresses National Standards for Arts Education, Music Grades K-4: 1b, 1e, 2b, 2d, 2f, 5a, 6b, 6c.

MATERIALS

- CD track 3 (with vocals); track 22 (accompaniment)
- CD player
- Songsheet or visual of music for each student
- Muffin cups (10 per group)
- Beans, macaroni, pennies or chips for counting
- Black marker

START

Introduce song with the following teaching strategy:

1. Teach the students a short rhythmic ostinato pattern by rote. Ask students to repeat after you as you tap on your legs L, R, L, R and say *"ti-ti-ti-ti"* (four eighth notes). Repeat several times, as students echo back. Next, slide your two palms together L hand forward, then back and say *"ta-a"* (one half note). Repeat several times, as students echo back. Put the two patterns together patting legs and sliding palms while you chant *"ti-ti-ti-ti ta-a."* Repeat several times, as students echo back. Check for student understanding and accuracy.

2. After students are very secure with the ostinato pattern with body percussion, play the recording of "Countdown to Christmas." Lead students as everyone performs the rhythmic ostinato while the music plays. Stop the ostinato when the counting begins. Repeat process several times.

DEVELOP

1. **ASK What do you think this song is about? How many days is it until Christmas (winter break, etc.)?**

2. Teach the words phrase by phrase, chanting each two-bar phrase in rhythm. Then, add the melody to the words, teaching two-bar phrases at a time.

3. Sing entire song with correct words, melody and rhythm. When secure, have students sing with the recording.

4. Add the rhythmic ostinato pattern learned earlier as the students sing with the recording. **ASK As you sing the song again, can you find places where the words match the rhythm of the ostinato pattern?** (Remember to stop the ostinato when the counting begins.)

5. Go to the board and write the ostinato pattern in stick notation. Have them read and chant the pattern (*"ti-ti-ti-ti ta-a"*).

6. Distribute copies of the songsheet. Lead students to circle or identify all the places they can find the repeating pattern (measures 2, 4, 6, 8, 10 and 12). Read and chant the pattern from the music.

7. Have students sing the song again with the recording while reading the music on the songsheet. Have them raise their hands each time they sing the *"ti-ti-ti-ti ta-a"* pattern.

EXTENDED ACTIVITIES

1. Sing other counting games such as "This Old Man," or "Ten in the Bed."

2. To reinforce counting, play a variety of counting games. Teacher claps three times, and children echo clap. **ASK How many times did you clap?** Repeat with different number of claps. Allow students to serve as leader. Vary the game with jumps, or snaps, or other body movement.

3. To reinforce counting backwards, prepare ten muffin papers or small cups with the numbers 1–10 written on the side or bottom in black marker. You may want to set up several small groups doing the same activity at the same time. Students are to count as they place a bean, penny, dry macaroni or chip in each cup – as many as to match the number on the side of the cup. For example, they are to place 5 beans in the cup labeled "5," counting each bean as they drop it into the cup. When they have filled the cups appropriately, they are then to remove the items, one at a time, counting backwards from the starting number on the side of the cup.

COUNTDOWN TO CHRISTMAS

2 measures introduction
Spirited (♩ = 120)

Words and Music by JOHN JACOBSON
and JANET DAY

Count - down to Christ - mas*, the best time of the year.

Count - down to Christ - mas, the sea - son of good cheer.

Can - dy canes and hol - ly and a spark - ling Christ - mas tree.

Lights up - on the house - top and a pres - ent just for me!

Count - down to Christ - mas, it's get - ting ve - ry near.

Count - down to Christ - mas, the best time of the year!

Students count backwards – days left until Christmas

10   9   8   (etc.)   Christ - mas time is here!

* OPTIONAL LYRICS for "Countdown to Winter"
Countdown to Winter, the best time of the year.
Countdown to Winter, the snow and fun are here.
Snowboarding, then skating by the snowy evergreen,
Sledding down the hillside, with hot chocolate in between.
Countdown to Winter, it's getting very near.
Countdown to Winter, the best time of the year!
10 9 8 7 6 5 4 3 2 1! Winter time is here!

Recording will include days 10 through 1. If using the accompaniment track on succeeding days, you can fill in the remaining beats with a long, sliding, "Ohhhh!" leading to "Christmas time is here!" For example, five days before the event: "5, 4, 3, 2, 1, Ohhhhhh, Christmas time is here!" Countdown will vary each day depending on the day started and the date of event.

Suggested Variations:
Countdown to CONCERT (countdown to the scheduled winter concert)
Countdown to RECESS (countdown to the scheduled winter break)
Countdown to WINTER (countdown to the first day of winter)
Countdown to SUMMER (countdown to last day of school)

THE DINOSAUR WALK

Lesson Plan by Ellen Shuler

LEARNING THROUGH
music

Let's explore the wonderful world of dinosaurs! Learn the names and characteristics of four dinosaurs in "The Dinosaur Walk." The possibilities are endless!

LESSON GOALS

- Keep a steady beat
- Learn the names and characteristics of four dinosaurs

This lesson addresses National Standards for Arts Education, Music Grades K-4: 1e, 2d, 6e.

MATERIALS

- CD track 4 (with vocals); track 23 (accompaniment)
- CD player
- Masking tape
- Dinosaur puppets or stuffed dinosaurs
- Books or posters on dinosaurs
- Art supplies (optional)

START

1. Introduce this song by discussing dinosaurs. Ask the students to name their favorite kind of dinosaurs. Show them pictures in books or on posters so that they can see what the different species look like.
2. Play the full performance recording of "The Dinosaur Walk." Have the children tap the steady beat while they listen to the words. During each verse, hold up a poster or point to a picture of the featured dinosaur.
3. Clap the syncopated rhythms in the song while speaking the text. Have the students repeat the rhythms back to you. (e.g., "Walk the walk," "talk the talk," "stomp the stomp," "Big and strong," "feet are huge" and "on the move.") Play the full performance recording again and have the children clap these syncopated rhythms when they occur in the song.

GAME

1. Make an alleyway by placing masking tape in two strips 4–6 feet apart on the floor. The length of the strips will vary by classroom size. Divide the class into two groups, each group standing in a line on a strip of tape facing the other.
2. During the Refrain, have each child keep a steady beat, changing the method with each Refrain (i.e. clapping, patsching, stomping).
3. One child or group is designated to be the dinosaur listed in each verse. He/She stomps down the walkway pretending to be that dinosaur during the appropriate Verse. You could also use dinosaur puppets, costumes, posters or pictures of each dinosaur as they stomp through the Dinosaur Walk.
4. Repeat until everyone has had a chance to go down the Dinosaur Walk.
5. Once the children are comfortable with the song and the movements, have them step away from the alleyway during each Refrain and invite them to stomp around the room to the steady beat while pretending to be their favorite dinosaur. Then find their spot on the alleyway for the walk-through.

EXTENDED ACTIVITIES

- Create dinosaur masks out of paper plates and elastic bands. Cut out holes for eyes and glue or staple the elastic band to hold the mask in place. Have the children draw and decorate their favorite dinosaur face.
- Make dinosaur feet out of old shoe boxes. Cut a small hole in one end of each box (large enough for a child's foot). Duck tape the box shut and stuff the inside with newspaper. Make sure you leave enough room for a child's foot. Spray paint or color the box. Add claws by gluing construction paper or fun foam to the top front of the box.
- Combine and create! These art projects can be done by the classroom teacher and brought to music class to enhance your lesson on dinosaurs.

THE DINOSAUR WALK

4 measures introduction

Prehistoric Allegro (♩ = 120)
Refrain

Words and Music by
JANET DAY

Let's all do the Din - o - saur Walk. We'll walk the walk___ and

talk the talk.___ We'll stomp the stomp___ on the Din - o - saur walk. So

(quasi foot stomps here)

let's all do the Din - o - saur Walk.

Verse

1. Here comes the T - Rex, big and strong.___ He on - ly eats meat and his

Verses 2, 3 & 4 see below

arms are not long. His roar is might - y and his feet are huge!___ Ty-

(quasi roar here)

ran - no - saur - us Rex is on the move!___

2. Pterodactylus, flying free,
   Over land and over sea,
   Wings that stretch from side to side.
   Pterodactylus cannot hide!

3. Welcome to Triceratops,
   Who has three horns upon his top.
   He lives among his family.
   Triceratops is something to see!

4. Here comes Stegasaurus now,
   Spikes from head to tail, wow!
   He only eats plants, so he won't hurt you.
   Stegasaurus is coming through!

HIGH LOW

Lesson Plan by Judy Herrington and Connie Schmidt

LEARNING THROUGH

Children explore pitch as infants and continue to be fascinated with vocal inflections as young children, including imitating cartoon characters, animal and nature sounds. Many children can match pitch at a very young age. Others acquire it through careful attention and practice. Learning to navigate the pitch spectrum is a major goal for young singers. This lesson helps students recognize and produce high and low pitches with speech, singing and instruments. The first steps involve careful listening. So get ears in gear!

LESSON GOALS

- Understand the music vocabulary of high and low
- Experience pitch differentiation
- Explore sounds produced with the voice

This lesson addresses National Standards for Arts Education, Music Grades K-4: 1b, 1e, 2e, 3a, 6c, 6e.

MATERIALS

- CD track 5 (with vocals); track 24 (accompaniment)
- CD player
- Copy of music for each singer (photocopy or overhead)
- Chart of vocal line shapes
- Orff instruments

START

Use vocal line shapes to explore high and low voice. Use different sounds to experience the effects (mmm, whoo, oo, whee, etc.) Trace the lines with your hand or a pencil varying the speed and the direction (it's fun to trace the line backwards). Experiment with the sound of a siren or the direction of a roller coaster. Suggested shapes:

DEVELOP

1. Introduce the song using song charts or overhead projection. Sing on "too" while pointing to notes on overhead or song chart. Sing in two-measure phrases, students echo.

2. Repeat process with words added.

3. Repeat without echo.
   Be aware that students often confuse high with soft and low with loud.

4. During the listening experience in mm. 17 to end, students respond to high pitches by reaching arms high above head; low pitches by reaching arms low to the ground; and middle pitches by clapping hands at chest and giggling.

EXTENDED ACTIVITIES

Melodic Direction

Draw arrows connecting the note heads. Identify the melodic direction of up, down or straight.

Sorting Project

"Can you find measures that are almost like mm. 1 and 2, 3 and 4 (uses the same interval but the rhythm is different).

Movement Interpretation

Using a set of scarves and piano improvisation, students can demonstrate high and low by moving the scarves appropriately. Use the black keys of the piano and the sustaining pedal to improvise melodies with simple harmonic accompaniments in the high range and the low range. Students interpret movement with the scarves high over their heads or close to the ground to correspond to the pitch of the melody.

Instrument exploration

Set up barred instruments in C pentatonic. For the listening section, use a student leader (or the teacher) to clap patterns above their head; students respond by playing high bars of their instrument (define the B bar as the divider). Or, assign glockenspiels to play with the high movement and basses to play with the low movement. Consider using large and small drums if there is a distinctive pitch variation; be sure to identify the high drum and the low drum.

HIGH LOW

8 measures introduction

Comical Sea Chantey (♩. = 108)

**Words and Music by JOHN JACOBSON
and JANET DAY**

Sing high, sing low. Let's play High Low.

5 Notes are high and notes are low and some are in the mid-dle.

9 When they're high, reach up high. When they're low, reach down low.

(3rd time)
Fine

13 When they're in the mid-dle, just clap your hands and gig-gle!

(repeat back to beginning 2 times)

Students listen to examples   *Students respond*   G7

17   *Repeat as desired**

If playing live, teacher or student leader provides high/low/middle samples.
  Recording has five examples in each verse.

IT'S RHYME TIME

Lesson Plan by Ellen Shuler

LEARNING THROUGH ■
music

Children of all ages use rhymes to play games, jump rope and memorize. In March, we celebrate the birthday of Dr. Seuss, the king of all rhymers, and this song is a wonderful tool to use with a classroom unit or review on rhyming words. Encourage students to focus not only on rhythmic accuracy but vowel and consonant sounds and syllables.

LESSON GOALS

- Sing a song in tune
- Understand rhyme scheme
- Expand students' knowledge of steady beat and rhythm
- Say rhyming words in rhythm

This lesson addresses National Standards for Arts Education, Music Grades K-4: 1e.

MATERIALS

- CD track 6 (with vocals); track 25 (accompaniment)
- CD player
- Chalk/markers and board
- Paper and pencils
- Books with rhymes – Dr. Seuss works great!
- Flash cards with rhyming words

START

1. Discuss what a rhyme is. Give examples. Ask the children for examples.
2. Review some favorite rhymes. These can be poems or lines from books.
3. Listen to "It's Rhyme Time." Have the children tap the steady beat while the song is playing.
4. Sing the song to the children. You may wish to write the rhyming words of the full performance track (#6) on the board or overhead and point to them as they listen.

DEVELOP

1. After singing the song, invite the children to come up with different words to try to rhyme.
2. Put the selected words on the board. Try to make a list of at least eight rhyming words.

3. Listen to the accompaniment track of "It's Rhyme Time" (track #25). Sing through the song again, this time using the new word list created by the class.

FOR OLDER STUDENTS

1. Divide the children into small groups. Give each group a piece of paper and a pencil. Have each group quietly make a list of eight rhyming words.
2. Sing along to the accompaniment track of "It's Rhyme Time." Invite one group to share their eight rhyming words in the first eight measures of the spoken rhyme section and then a different group to take the second eight measures of the spoken rhyme section. Repeat the song until every group has a chance to share.

FLASH CARD CHALLENGE

1. Create flash cards with rhyming words on them. You will need eight in a set (i.e. seven words that rhyme with "cat" etc.)
2. During the spoken section, hold up the cards and have the students read the rhyming words in rhythm.
3. Variation: Create a flip book where the last syllable remains the same (e.g. "at") and only the first letter or letters change (e.g. "c" "ch") to create the rhyming words. Have the students read the flipbook words in rhythm to the spoken section of the song.

CREATIVE CHALLENGE

1. Seat the class in a circle.
2. Select a word for the class to rhyme, but do not share it with the class. Play the accompaniment track of the song. On the first measure of the spoken rhyme, speak the word you have selected. On the second measure have the student on your right rhyme with your word. Continue around the circle with every measure having students select different words to rhyme with your word! On the repeat, select a new word and continue around the circle where the students left off. Sing through the song until every student gets a chance to rhyme with one of your words!

IT'S RHYME TIME

Words and Music by JANET DAY

4 measures introduction

More Rhyming Words

dog	pop	pay	bell	sing
log	cop	day	tell	ring
fog	bop	say	fell	wing
jog	top	nay	shell	king
hog	mop	hay	sell	swing
bog	drop	ray	spell	thing
frog	flop	play	yell	bring
cog	crop	bay	well	spring

JANUARY FRIENDS

Lesson Plan by Judy Herrington and Connie Schmidt

LEARNING THROUGH
music

January = a new year + resolutions. Take a few quiet moments to reset your teaching goals. What has worked well so far this year? Would you like to change anything?

Assessment is not only for our students, but is a constant process for us to evaluate our own teaching and its effectiveness. At this point in the school year, routines are well established, relationships with students and teachers are secure, and new skills have been added and practiced. This can be a valuable time to give students an opportunity to sing alone or in small groups.

Use "January Friends/February Friends" as a method to help meet this goal. Solo/small group singing enables a child to more easily hear him or herself AND allows the teacher to assess pitch-matching skill at the same time. Use this and many other singing games and activities to help build independent singers.

Additionally, there are a surprising number of American holidays and birthdates of historical figures in the first two months of the year. Add your own local school figures by including birth months of students in your class as well as the school staff. This could be the catalyst for new camaraderie among students and adults based upon birthdates. Happy New Year!

LESSON GOALS
- Sing in tune
- Steady beat
- Uneven/even rhythm patterns (syncopation)
- Melodic direction
- Melodic sequences

This lesson addresses National Standards for Arts Education, Music Grades K-4: 1a, 1b, 1e, 2f, 6b, 6c.

MATERIALS
- CD tracks 7 & 8 (with vocals); track 26 (accompaniment)
- CD player
- Copy of music for each singer (photocopy or overhead)
- Hand percussion instruments

START
1. Establish a soft patschen beat; teacher speaks words rhythmically, students echo. Be sure to accent the syncopation.
2. Repeat speaking together and clapping the rhythm of the words simultaneously.
3. Repeat using clap only ("put the words inside your head"). Identify like and unlike rhythm patterns. It can be fun to have one half the class patschen the steady beat, and the other half clap the rhythm of the words.

DEVELOP
Introduce the melody and accent the syncopation. It can be helpful for students to touch the notes as they are singing. This also gives the teacher the opportunity to observe if students are tracking properly.

EXTENDED ACTIVITIES
- Have students clap odd numbered measures, and sing even numbered measures. Reverse— sing odd numbered measures, clap even numbered measures.
- Divide class into three groups:
  Group 1: sing measures 1 & 2
  Group 2: sing measures 3 & 4
  Group 3: sing measures 5 & 6
  All groups: sing 7 & 8 and refrain.
  Follow the same process using individual students or small groups to sing sections.
- Identify rests in the music. Add a percussion instrument in place of the rest. Be sure to give all students a turn! Add a soft steady beat with hand drums plus the "surprise" instruments on the rests.

FOR OLDER STUDENTS
- Can your class organize a line based on birthdays (January through December)? Students who have the same month birthdays should stand side by side. Write a timeline of class birthdays on the board or large tag board.
- Create a chant to be used between verses:
  "We are January friends" *(Speak January-born students' names, each name followed by two claps.)* Continue with other months.
  End with: "The fun just never ends!" *(clap, clap)*

JANUARY FRIENDS

4 measures introduction

**Words and Music by JOHN JACOBSON
and JANET DAY**

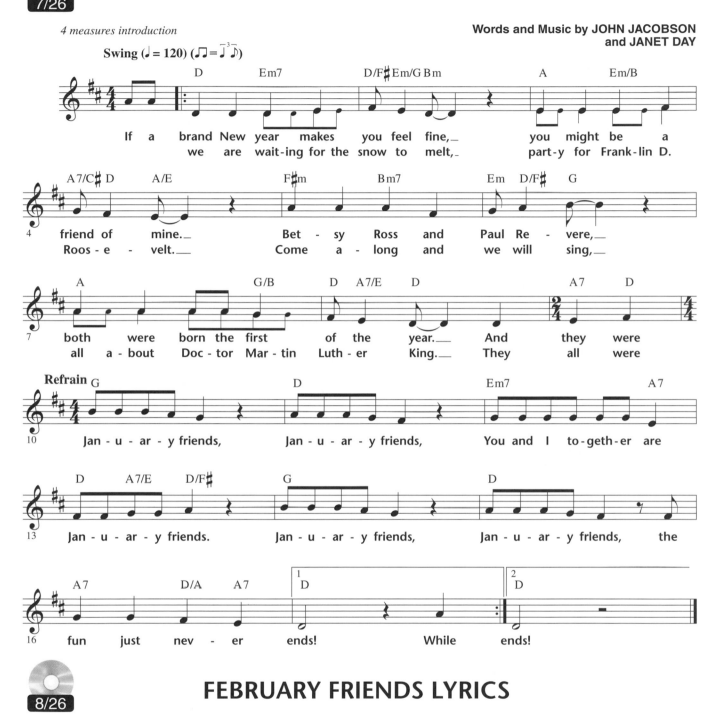

Swing (♩ = 120)

If a brand New year makes you feel fine,___ you might be a
we are wait-ing for the snow to melt,___ a part-y for Frank-lin D.

friend of mine.___ Bet - sy Ross and Paul Re - vere,___
Roos - e - velt.___ Come a - long and we will sing,___

both were born the first of the year.___ And they were
all a - bout Doc - tor Mar - tin Luth - er King.___ They all were

Refrain

Jan - u - ar - y friends, Jan - u - ar - y friends, You and I to-geth-er are

Jan - u - ar - y friends. Jan - u - ar - y friends, Jan - u - ar - y friends, the

fun just nev - er ends! While ends!

FEBRUARY FRIENDS LYRICS

1. If you like groundhogs or valentines,
Super Bowl Sunday from the scrimmage line,
With President's Day, you can't go wrong,
Come, join us now and sing along.
Because we're February friends, February friends,
You and I together are February friends.
February friends, February friends,
The fun just never ends!

2. There's African American history,
Ev'ry four years another day for me.
Birthdays for Reagan, Lincoln, Washington,
Don't forget William Henry Harrison.
Oh, they're all February friends, February friends,
You and I together are February friends.
February friends, February friends,
The fun just never ends!

MY FRIENDS ARE ALL AROUND

Lesson Plan by Judy Herrington and Connie Schmidt

LEARNING THROUGH
music

The beginning of a new school year may cause excitement or worry, but with friends and comrades, the venture becomes fun! Friends know each others' names. Help your students become a community more rapidly by teaching their names. Worries ease, rough edges are smoothed, classroom management is improved – all by the simple act of using individual names. Calling a child by name quickly validates and builds teacher/student and student/student communication. Use "My Friends Are All Around" and its related rhythm activities to lay a fine basis for a year of "whole child" learning.

LESSON GOALS

- Learn names of students
- Learn and demonstrate steady beat
- Encourage 'solo' opportunities
- If using percussion instruments, opportunity to reinforce proper playing technique and care of instruments.

This lesson addresses National Standards for Arts Education, Music Grades K-4: 1b, 1e, 2a, 2f, 4b, 5d, 6b, 6c.

MATERIALS

- CD track 9 (with vocals); track 27 (accompaniment)
- CD player
- Word/lyric chart with song printed or notated, large enough for the class to see easily.
- Flashcards with students' names or name tags

START

1. Introduce song with the word/lyric chart.
2. Teacher speaks and students echo, phrase by phrase; keep steady beat using patschen, or other body percussion or hand drum.
3. Class and teacher speak the entire song in rhythm. Continue to maintain steady pulse.
4. Repeat the same process adding the melody. Draw attention to like and unlike phrases.

DEVELOP

1. To introduce and ensure quick success, the teacher speaks child's name (note: be sure to check on pronunciation before starting the game) and the class claps back the rhythm of the names.
2. When the process is secure, students speak their own name in turn and clap the rhythm of their name (teacher should use non-verbal cues to indicate their entrance).
3. When secure on rhythm of names and clapping, try performing with CD accompaniment track #27. Teacher will point to first child in group of four and child will speak name on beat and clap the rhythm of his/her name on beat where indicated. The accompaniment track on the CD is repeated two times allowing room for eight names. Repeat track until all children get a chance to perform with the CD accompaniment.

EXTENDED ACTIVITIES

- Substitute "play" for clap and use a percussion instrument. Depending on the skill and availability of instruments, the students can pass the instrument around the circle or the teacher holds the instrument and a mallet is passed from student to student.
- Experiment with combinations of speech and percussion patterns for the speech/name section. For example, students are seated in circle.

  "Say your name" _____
  (students say the rhythm of their names)

  "Play your name"_____
  (students play the rhythm of their names)

  "Pass it on"
  (pass the instrument on to the next student; class continues a steady pulse patschen until the next student is ready to play.)

FOR OLDER STUDENTS

Randomly place students in groups of three to five in each. Students create a rhythm pattern using their names. Transfer rhythms to body percussion or percussion instruments and perform for class. Stack these rhythm patterns together and replace in the speech section of the "My Friends Are All Around" song.

MY FRIENDS ARE ALL AROUND

Words and Music by JOHN JACOBSON
and JANET DAY

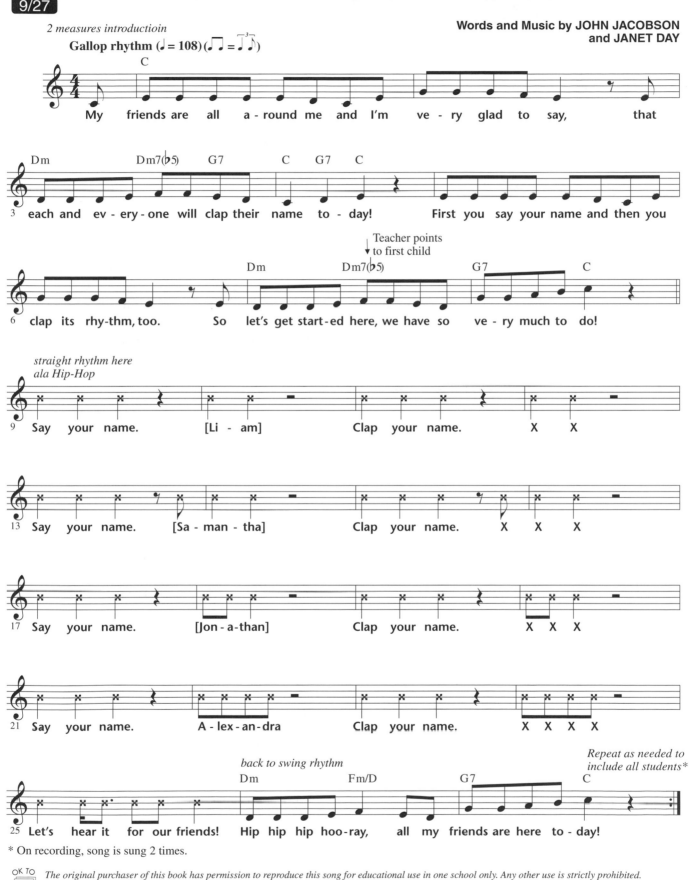

2 measures introductioin

Gallop rhythm (♩ = 108)

C
My friends are all a-round me and I'm ve-ry glad to say, that

Dm **Dm7(♭5)** **G7** **C** **G7** **C**
each and ev-ery-one will clap their name to-day! First you say your name and then you

Teacher points
to first child

Dm **Dm7(♭5)** **G7** **C**
clap its rhy-thm, too. So let's get start-ed here, we have so ve-ry much to do!

*straight rhythm here
ala Hip-Hop*

Say your name. [Li - am] Clap your name. X X

Say your name. [Sa - man - tha] Clap your name. X X X

Say your name. [Jon - a - than] Clap your name. X X X

Say your name. A - lex - an - dra Clap your name. X X X X

back to swing rhythm   *Repeat as needed to
include all students**

Dm **Fm/D** **G7** **C**
Let's hear it for our friends! Hip hip hip hoo-ray, all my friends are here to-day!

* On recording, song is sung 2 times.

MY VERY EDUCATED MOM JUST SERVED US NINE PIES

Lesson Plan by Judy Herrington and Connie Schmidt

LEARNING THROUGH
music

Here's a chance to take your music classes right out of this world! Your Language Arts and Science teachers will appreciate this playful tune as well. Acronyms, vocabulary, astronomy, vocal range and rhythm—enjoy them all and remember; the sky's the limit!

LESSON GOALS

- Sing in tune
- Introduce and practice major/minor intervals
- Experiment with percussion accompaniments
- Learn planet names
- Explore acronyms

This lesson addresses National Standards for Arts Education, Music Grades K-4: 1b, 1e, 2a, 2f, 3d, 4b, 4c, 6b, 6c.

MATERIALS

- CD track 10 (with vocals); track 28 (accompaniment)
- CD player
- Copy of music for each singer (photocopy or overhead)
- Word chart of planet names, first letter in caps
- Percussion instruments

START

1. Explain acronyms and mnemonic learning techniques and how they are utilized in this piece. (The 1st letter of each word in the title is also the 1st letter of each planet, in order closest to and moving away from the sun.)
2. Teacher speaks and students echo song, phrase by phrase; keep steady beat using patschen. Speak clearly and rhythmically.
3. Class and teacher speak the entire piece in rhythm. Continue to maintain steady pulse.
4. Repeat the same process adding the melody.

DEVELOP

1. Draw attention to syncopation by speaking m. 6 ("-fore your eyes") in straight rhythm with students echoing. Repeat, with syncopation and accents on the syncopated words.
2. Address specific intervals in the song (i.e. octave).

EXTENDED ACTIVITIES

- Use the B section for solo or small group singing opportunities.
- Add percussion for special effects, such as thunder tube and/or drum roll for the introduction. In the B section, use a different percussion instrument to be played on each letter name.
- *Science Note. Ask your science teacher about the astronomical discoveries regarding the planet Pluto. Should you want to sing the song without including Pluto, the words of the text can be changed. Feel free to sing "Neckties" instead of "Nine Pies." Then replace Pluto phrase in the B section with "such are the wonders that orbit the skies."
- Create a rhythm ostinato piece using the planet names in combination. Determine the rhythmic patterns, combining two or more planet names (it's fun to include rests or syncopation). Transfer to percussion instruments. Stack the patterns.

FOR OLDER STUDENTS

- Draw attention to the flat that changes the mode to a minor key. Repeat the section without the flat to experience the contrast of major and minor.
- Create alliteration speech rhythms using the first letter of each planet. For example.

    Merry, moody, mighty Mercury
    Joyful, jazzy jivin' Jupiter

  Use these alliterations spoken rhythmically and layered for a speech ensemble. Transfer to percussion instruments. This can become the middle section of a performance using the melody, My Very Educated Mom (A) plus the speech patterns (B) and the return of the melody (A).
- Create your own acronym poem using adjectives to describe planetary objects. For example: (COMET) Colorful Orbiting Mystical Energy Tail.

Other possibilities: Star, Meteor, Moon, Space

MY VERY EDUCATED MOM JUST SERVED US NINE PIES

Words and Music by JOHN JACOBSON
and JANET DAY

2 measures introduction and interlude

Celestial Pop Rock (♩ = 116)

*See alternate lyric suggestions in lesson plan.

PENGUINS AND POLAR BEARS

Lesson Plan by Ellen Shuler

When the holiday season arrives, it's time to celebrate snowballs, snowflakes, penguins and polar bears! This clever winter song is a great piece to teach geography by identifying the North and South Pole, and beginning part-singing. Ideal for holiday/winter concerts, the three-part layered harmony in "Penguins and Polar Bears" is very accessible to even the youngest children.

LESSON GOALS

- Sing a song in tune
- Sing in layered harmony
- Connect music with disciplines outside the arts

This lesson addresses National Standards for Arts Education, Music Grades K-4: 1b, 1d, 1e, 8b.

MATERIALS

- CD track 11 (with vocals); track 29 (accompaniment)
- CD player
- Chalk/markers and board
- Globe

START

1. Discuss polar bears and penguins. How are they the same? (live in cold climate, good swimmers) How they are different? (size, color, mouths, penguins are birds and live in the South Pole whereas polar bears are mammals and live in the North Pole) Rarely do their paths cross, except in this funny song.

2. Listen to the song, having students tap a steady beat. Teacher taps a steady beat on a globe, tapping the North Pole when the word "polar bear" is mentioned, and tapping the South Pole when the word "penguin" is mentioned.

3. Listen and instruct children to lower hands towards the floor when they hear the word "penguin" (South Pole), and raise their hands over their heads when they hear the word "polar bear" (North Pole). Repeat several times.

4. Invite students to sing through "Penguins and Polar Bears." (Teacher may continue with the lowering and raising of arms.)

DEVELOP

1. Teacher draws a large "1, 2, 3" on the board. Explain that there are three sections to this song. Have students stand on first verse (teacher points to "1"), sit on second verse (teacher points to "2"), and march in place on third verse (teacher points to "3").

2. Divide the class into three groups. Have each group stand in a separate area of the room. Play the recording again, and this time have group 1 sing the first verse, group 2 sing the second verse and group 3 sing the third verse. Check that all students are singing in tune.

REVIEW AND PERFORM

1. After practicing the verses separately, have students sing the three verses together at the same time.

2. Practice several times until students are able to sing the layered harmony accurately.

PERFORMANCE OPPORTUNITY

"Penguins and Polar Bears" would be a great addition to a holiday/winter concert as a combined piece for different grades. You can assign the three verses to different grade levels. At the concert, impress the parents by singing all parts together on the final verse of the song!

ASSESS

- Did the students sing in tune?
- Did the students sing the layered harmony accurately?
- Can students identify things that are the same and things that are different between penguins and polar bears?

PENGUINS AND POLAR BEARS

Words and Music by JOHN JACOBSON

SAFETY FIRST!

Lesson Plan by Charyl Granatella

LEARNING THROUGH
music

From flashing lights on shoes to school safety cadets, from fire drills to hallway safety, we can take nothing for granted. We teach how to drink from a water fountain, how to walk down the stairs, how to walk "with the light" how to walk "facing traffic" and how to keep our shoelaces tied. Everything is easier to teach when we have a positive attitude and a memorable song.

LESSON GOALS

- Sing and play the interval of a falling third: sol-mi, G-E
- Sing and play the melodic pattern mi-re-do, E-D-C
- Identify Introduction and Verse and Refrain in song form
- Learn all the verses and create more
- Play simple percussion instruments to the rhythm of the song
- Recognize two different timbres between sticks and triangles (or finger cymbals)

This lesson addresses National Standards for Arts Education, Music Grades K-4: 1b, 1e, 2b, 5b, 6a.

MATERIALS

- CD track 12 (with vocals); track 30 (accompaniment)
- CD player
- Small diatonic bells
- Prepared chart or chalkboard with following: so-so-mi (with hand signs or words) or pitch names G-G-E or all
- Prepared chart or chalkboard with mi-mi-re-re-do (with hand signs or words) or pitch names E-E-D-D-C or all
- Prepared chart or chalkboard with vocabulary words: Verse and Refrain, interval, scale, descending
- Small hand percussion instruments

START

Warm up children by singing:

1. Echo-sing and sign using the pentatonic scale intervals and solfége.
   - So-So-So-La
   - So-La-So
   - So-Mi-Do
   - Fa-Fa-Fa-So-La-La-So-Fa (Advanced Second Grade)
   - Mi-Re-Do
   - Do-Re-Mi
2. End warm-up with the "Falling Third" So-Mi

Warm up children by clapping:

1. Echo-clap some basic easy rhythms. Choose excerpts from the song.
2. Clap quarter notes (ta) and patschen half notes (ta-ah) as you continue with more rhythms.
3. Listen to the entire song (4 verses and Refrain). Each time the Verse in sung, have children tap steady beat on lap. During the Refrain, have children perform the rhythm of the words (clap quarter notes and patschen half notes).

DEVELOP

1. Lead a discussion on the importance of personal safety. Brainstorm various safety measures that they have in their lives. Make a chart. These may include: lights on shoes, night lights, Safety Cadets and School Crossing Guards, traffic signals and crosswalks, fire frills at school and at home.
2. Listen again to the song. Have children listen for safety actions mentioned to add to your Safety List. Write them on the board as the children offer them up. (Wear a helmet while riding one's bike, never talk to strangers, don't stand on the swings, don't walk up the slide, take care when crossing streets, know your phone number and street address, always wear a seatbelt.
3. Play the song and have the children sing the Refrain. Add ringing percussion to the half note words. Play again, singing the words; play the quarter notes of the Refrain with rhythm sticks.

SAFETY FIRST!

Country 2-beat (♩ = 120)

Words and Music by JOHN JACOBSON
and JANET DAY

When I go out rid - ing, my hel - met's on my head. I
Play - ing on the swing - set, I nev - er stand, I sit. My

Verses 3 & 4 see below

nev - er talk to strang - ers, I just walk a - way in - stead.
feet go first on down the slide, a per - fect safe - ty fit.

Refrain

Safe - ty first! Safe - ty first! We'll have lots of

fun if we put safe - ty first! Safe - ty first! Safe - ty first!

We'll live long and hap - py if we all put safe - ty first!

first!

all put safe - ty first!_____

(new key)
3. Crossing streets, I'm careful; I play nice on recess.
   I memorize my phone number and know my home address.
   Refrain
4. Always wear a seatbelt when riding in a car
   and never, ever swim alone, no matter who you are!
   Refrain to Coda

SAY HELLO WHEREVER YOU GO   25

SAY HELLO WHEREVER YOU GO

Lesson Plan by Judy Herrington and Connie Schmidt

LEARNING THROUGH
music

Whether at the beginning of the school term or throughout the year, greet your students in several languages with this bright, happy tune.

LESSON GOALS

- Learn "hello" greetings in many languages
- Recognize like and unlike phrases
- Experience echo-singing as the echo and as the leader
- Learn names of students and classmates

This lesson addresses National Standards for Arts Education, Music Grades K-4: 1a, 1b, 1e, 2a, 2d, 6a.

MATERIALS

- CD track 13 (with vocals); track 31 (accompaniment)
- CD player
- Song chart or overhead projection of melody and words
- Visual of music for each student
- Variety of hand percussion instruments

START

Introduce the song with one of two teaching strategy options:

Teaching Strategy: Option 1

1. It can be a valuable challenge for young singers to read and work from a score. Use either a song chart, overhead projection, or a copy of the song for each student. **ASK Can you clap two times whenever I sing "Hello"?** Give singers a moment to look ahead to find where "hello" comes in the score. Sing the song; students clap two beats for "hello" each time it occurs. Stop at the end of m.13.

2. **ASK Can you pat the rhythm of "I want to say" on your knees?** (patschen) Repeat above process; sing the song using patschen ("I want to say") and clapping ("hello"). Usually, students are singing the melody by this time.

Teaching Strategy: Option 2

1. Establish the beat by lightly tapping knees; invite students to tap with you and to echo you as you speak the words in rhythm (mm. 5-14).

   Teacher: "I want to say Hello wherever I go."
   Students echo: "I want to say Hello wherever I go."

2. Repeat the process with students echo-singing each phrase.

DEVELOP

1. Using the song chart or overhead projection, identify the sections of "Say Hello Wherever You Go." **ASK Do you notice what happens to the melody each time you sing the words "I want to say Hello"?** (The phrases are alike.)

2. Teach the rest of the song (mm. 14 to end). Identify "Leader" and "Echo" parts. Explain 1st and 2nd endings and repeat signs. Sing the song assuming the role of leader in mm.14-21 as students echo you. Repeat the song, only this time, invite the class to sing the leader's part as you sing the echo.

EXTENDED ACTIVITIES

- Explore language possibilities. Ask students to discover the "hello" greeting from their family's country of origin. Use the various greetings in the song.

- Play a Name Game. The formation is a seated circle. Establish a steady beat (patschen). The first student says, "My name is Sarah." The class replies, "Hola, Sarah." Continue around the circle as each student says his/her name and is greeted by the class. For a final challenge, have the class speak, in order, the names of all students in the circle while using a patsch-clap ostinato, e.g. Hola, Sarah. Hola, Miguel. Hola, Nick. etc. Change to a different body percussion ostinato the next day.

- Vary the game in the following ways: (1) Use a different language. (2) After greeting everyone in the circle, have students change places. Can the class remember everyone's name in the reconfigured circle?

SAY HELLO WHEREVER YOU GO

Words and Music by JOHN JACOBSON
and JANET DAY

SEASONS 'ROUND AND ROUND

Lesson Plan by Judy Herrington and Connie Schmidt

LEARNING THROUGH
music

Holidays and seasons give order to a young child's life in that their concept of time is developing. Each teacher is encouraged to discuss seasons by using the weather or holidays as appropriate to their geographic region.

LESSON GOALS

- Learn order of the seasons
- Experience part-singing (round)
- Experience Orff instrument ostinato accompaniment
- Develop music vocabulary: octave, round, glissando, (for extended activities: dynamics—piano, forte, mezzo-piano, mezzo-forte)

This lesson addresses National Standards for Arts Education, Music Grades K-4: 1b, 1d, 1e, 2a, 2d, 2f, 6e.

MATERIALS

- CD track 14 (with vocals); track 32 (accompaniment)
- CD player
- Song Chart or overhead projection of melody and words
- Props; scarves or streamers (see below)
- Orff instruments

START

1. Clap the text in rhythm by 2-measure phrases with students echoing. Be sure to give clear gestures for the rest.
2. Sing on "loo" and point to notes on overhead or song chart. Sing in 2-measure phrases, students echo.
3. Repeat process with words added.
4. Repeat without echo.

DEVELOP

Add barred instrument part

1. Teach pattern by rote, indicating that we are playing an octave starting on the high note. The piece ends with a glissando on the last 'fall.'

2. A 2-measure instrument ostinato can be used for an introduction and interlude.

Sing in a round

1. Review song in unison without assistance from the teacher.
2. Challenge students to sing independently while the teacher sings something different (round). Ask students to describe what they observed.
3. The teacher requests several students "to help" with part 2. Be sure to place group with space between.
4. Divide class in half with space between sections.
5. Trade parts.

Performance Possibility

2-measure introduction with instrument ostinato unison melody

2-measure instrument interlude

2-part round, sung twice

EXTENDED ACTIVITIES

- If you have a class set of scarves, students can experiment moving with scarves while singing the song in unison. Have students take turns being a leader with students simultaneously copying movement. End the song with a swirl and fall. (A substitute prop might be streamers attached to popsicle sticks or tongue depressors.)

- Introducing dynamics with the following process can be helpful and fun:

The teacher holds hands palm to palm, fingertips pointing forward. **SAY This shows you to sing soft—it's also called *piano*.** Students copy simultaneously.

The teacher holds hands palm to palm, shoulder distance apart. **SAY This shows you to sing loud (not shouting)—it's called *forte*.**

The teacher then conducts the volume with the above signals for soft and loud while the song is sung in unison.

After this is secure, add graduations of dynamic levels (mp, mf) indicating and identified by the space between hands.

- Consider singing in the keys of "D" and "E" to extend and experience head voice.

SEASONS 'ROUND AND ROUND

Words and Music by JOHN JACOBSON
Arranged by JANET DAY

Copyright © 2007 by HAL LEONARD CORPORATION
International Copyright Secured   All Rights Reserved

THE SHADOW OF A GROUNDHOG

Lesson Plan by Charyl Granatella

LEARNING THROUGH
music

Everybody loves Groundhog Day! It's full of hope and imagination as we venerate the furry mammal of weather lore. Centuries ago, Europeans watched for hibernating mammals to signal winter's end. Now it is an American and Canadian holiday and this little tune is a great vehicle to reinforce steady beat and la-based pentachords. (A pentachord is a five-note segment of a scale.)

LESSON GOALS

- Maintain a steady beat
- Play a steady beat ostinato with a rest
- Hear the difference in the *do* pentachord and the *la* pentachord and sing them
- Sing up the scale; see an ascending scale passage
- Develop inner hearing
- Have fun with a long and fun tradition of Groundhog Day
- Discussion of seasons, weather, folk lore

This lesson addresses National Standards for Arts Education, Music Grades K-4: 1b, 1e, 2a, 2f, 5b, 6b, 6c.

MATERIALS

- CD track 15 (with vocals); track 33 (accompaniment)
- CD player
- Small hand percussion optional
- Visual of
- Visual of *do* pentachord (*do re mi fa so*)
- Visual of *la* pentachord (*la ti do re mi*)
- Visual of the title "The Shadow of a Groundhog"
- A monthly calendar

START

1. Warm up your children by singing:
   a. Sing various *do* pentachords, singing the words "going up the scale" and have them gesture with their hands in an upward motion.

   b. Switch to *la* pentachords (minor tonality) and change the phrase to "sing a different scale." Use a hushed and dramatic voice to emphasize the change in mood. **ASK Does this sound happy or sad?** Make sure to sing the Dm pentachord pattern from beginning of song. (D, E, F, G, A)

2. Warm up your children by clapping:
   a. Echo-clap some basic easy rhythms.
   b. Have the children repeat the pattern by patting or clapping (ostinato).
   c. Write the pattern on the board or have a prepared visual.
   d. Play the song "The Shadow of a Groundhog" while the children pat the ostinato.

DEVELOP

1. Tell the children the title of the song and ask them to list some Groundhog Day facts, such as: It occurs on February 2nd. He looks for his shadow. He predicts six more weeks of winter, or not.

2. Have the children speak the first phrase of Verse 1 (in rhythm) "On Feb-ru-ar-y sec-ond, be-hold, the ground-hog steps out-side, I'm told." Check diction and pronunciation, especially of February. Do the same for the second verse.

3. Ask the children to listen for places in the music where they could sing "sing a different scale." *(la pentachord)*

4. Have the children make the gesture for the ascending scale when it occurs (seven times – m. 4, 8, 17, 23, 8, 17, 24).

5. Teach the song (phrase by phrase).

6. Divide the class in half; have one group sing the song while the other group plays the ostinato from the warm-up on small hand percussion. Then switch.

EXTENDED ACTIVITY:

Using the calendar, find February 2nd. Count ahead six weeks, to March 16th. Keep track of the weather and make a decision what conditions would make it Spring. Was the groundhog in your area accurate?

THE SHADOW OF A GROUNDHOG

Words and Music by JOHN JACOBSON
and JANET DAY

THE SPELLING BEE

Lesson Plan by Ellen Shuler

LEARNING THROUGH
music

Your kids will be "buzzing" about spelling bees with this song. *The Spelling Bee* is a wonderful song to help students learn not only to spell, but also to incorporate musical skills into this fun activity!

LESSON GOALS

- Keep a steady beat
- Spell three and four-letter words in rhythm
- Learn *sol fa mi re do*, downward musical phrase
- Participate in call and response
- Learn beginning rhythm patterns and reading

This lesson addresses National Standards for Arts Education, Music Grades K-4: 1b, 1e, 5a, 6b, 6c .

MATERIALS

- CD track 16 (with vocals); track 34 (accompaniment)
- CD player
- Bumblebee puppet or stuffed animal
- Chalk/markers and board
- Spelling flash cards

START

1. Ask the children about spelling bees. Talk about the different aspects of a spelling bee. Kids are given words to spell and can ask for definitions, word origins, and for the word to be used in a sentence. In every round, the words get harder to spell.

2. Introduce the class to your "Spelling Bee" puppet. If you have a bee puppet, wonderful! If not, it is easy to make one from a black sock and yellow construction paper, felt or fleece. You could also find a Bumblebee stuffed animal at your local toy store.

3. Before listening to the song, have the children sing a descending scale pattern, *sol fa mi re do*. Describe this downward musical line as the sound a bee makes when it lands on a flower. Tell the children to listen for this melody line in "The Spelling Bee."

4. Play the song "The Spelling Bee" and have the children listen and tap the steady beat on their laps.

5. Invite the children to sing along with the parts marked "students" as you play the full performance again. Encourage them to keep the steady beat. The teacher should be the leader with the help of the "Spelling Bee" puppet and the children should respond with the letters.

6. Have the children identify the sections of the song that follow the descending pattern of *sol fa mi re do.* ("use my A B Cs," and "Help me, spelling bee!") Hand raising or standing/sitting each time they hear it is a great way for them to demonstrate this.

DEVELOP

1. During the buzzing section, have the students buzz around the room like a swarm of bees, reminding them that the bees must sing!

2. Have the children stop moving on the last *sol fa mi re do* measure: ("Help me, Spelling Bee!") Have them show with their bodies the downward scale movement. Have an area where the buzzing bees can land (such as a rug or carpet squares) and call it the flower. This also helps to focus the class on the spelling task ahead!

3. Have the "Spelling Bee" puppet lead the children in spelling the words in the song. Have the entire class spell together. For the younger grades, use flash cards and point to each letter. You may also want to try this without the CD accompaniment at a slower tempo until the children get used to spelling the words. For older grades, add music notation to the letter rhythms.

4. Invite the students to take turns being the leader and using the "Spelling Bee" puppet. Have the students say the spelling words for the class.

VARIATION

Ask the classroom teachers for a list of spelling words that the students are learning. Incorporate these words into the song. Make sure to fit the words in rhythmically.

THE SPELLING BEE

Words and Music by JOHN JACOBSON
and JANET DAY

2 measures introduction
Easy walking tempo (♩ = ca. 92) *(straight eighths)*

Here comes the spell-ing bee, help-ing to spell words you see.

Here comes the spell-ing bee, let's use our A B C's.

Here comes my spell-ing bee, help-ing me spell words I see.

Here comes my spell-ing bee, I'll use my A B C's.

Buzz buzz buzz buzz buzz buzz buzz buzz buzz buzz buzz buzz buzz buzz buzz buzz

buzz buzz buzz buzz buzz buzz buzz buzz. Help me, spell-ing bee!

Leader:	Students:	Leader:	Students:
Spell the word YES.	Y E S	Spell the word NO.	N O
Spell the word RED.	R E D	Spell the word BLUE.	B L U E
Spell the word THE.	T H E	Spell the word THEY.	T H E Y

Leader:	Students:	Leader:	Students:
Spell the word STOP.	S T O P	Spell the word GO.	G O
Spell the word OLD.	O L D	Spell the word NEW.	N E W
Spell the word SING.	S I N G	Spell the word SAY.	S A Y

N.C. (back to original feel)   1, 2 G7   3 G7   C Cadd9   *(go directly to zz)*

Now we're spell-ing bees! Buzz____

THESE ARE THE MONTHS OF THE YEAR

Lesson Plan by Ellen Shuler

LEARNING THROUGH
music

Teaching the months of the year with a song is a wonderful way to reinforce student learning through the arts, and to promote cross-curricular study with the classroom teachers.

LESSON GOALS

- Name and recognize the months of the year
- Sing in tune and with accurate rhythms
- Feel the beat in a 3-beat pattern
- Reinforce learning through the arts

This lesson addresses National Standards for Arts Education, Music Grades K-4: 1a, 1b, 1e, 2a, 6a.

MATERIALS

- CD track 17 (with vocals); track 35 (accompaniment)
- CD player
- Poster board or paper
- Crayons or markers

START

1. Ask students to name the month of the year in which their birthday occurs. Introduce the song by asking students to stand in place when they hear the month of their birthday. Teacher then chants in rhythm the first section of the song (A Section, measures 1-16), with students standing as they hear their birthday month. Teacher chants song again, but this time having students sit down when they hear their birthday month.

2. To help students feel the beat in groups of 3, introduce a simple three-beat body percussion pattern such as clap, clap, snap or pat, clap, snap. Repeat several times. Then teach the A Section by echo-chanting in four-bar phrases. Teacher chants four bars in rhythm (while doing the three-beat body percussion pattern) and students echo. Repeat several times until children can recite the months of the year in rhythm to the song while performing the 3-beat body percussion pattern.

3. Play the recording of "These Are the Months of the Year." Ask students if they heard anything new? (B section) Teach students to sing both the A and B sections by rote and/or with recording.

DEVELOP

Set up workstations in the room (use floor area or hallway). Divide class into groups of four or five, preferably by birthday month. For example, October birthdays in one group and so forth. Assign each group a month and plan for at least one group per month. Distribute poster board or art paper, markers or crayons to each group. Have each group design a poster for their assigned month that includes the month name and one or more activities associated with the month (including the birthdays). For younger students, teacher may write month names on posters in advance. Teacher may play recording of song while students work on posters.

REINFORCE

When calendar posters are complete, have students sing the song and invite a representative of each group to hold up the poster at the appropriate time. Select other students to play rhythm instruments in a three-beat pattern during the instrumental interlude.

VARIATIONS

Divide the song into four-bar phrases (eight in all). Encourage independent singing by inviting small groups of singers to sing each four-bar phrase. Eventually, ask soloists to sing each four-bar phrase alone. Check for good intonation in singing and accurate rhythms.

Encourage students to create three-beat patterns with body instruments (pat, tap, clap, stomp) or with rhythm band instruments. Have students play their patterns during the instrumental interlude.

THESE ARE THE MONTHS OF THE YEAR

4 measures introduction

Words and Music by
JANET DAY

*(Second time is instrumental interlude to letter B. Each child names their favorite month and why.
Repeat until all children have had the opportunity to share.)*

Copyright © 2007 by HAL LEONARD CORPORATION
International Copyright Secured   All Rights Reserved

WE CAN-CAN BE HEALTHY KIDS

Lesson Plan by Charyl Granatella

LEARNING THROUGH
music

Little people are very teachable and need to learn good health and safety habits early. How better to teach them than through a rousing dance routine!

LESSON GOALS

- Perform gross motor movements on the beat
- Memorize choreography
- Introduce (or review) quarter notes *(ta)* and eighth notes *(ti-ti)*
- Learn (or review) two-part song form (AB); learn or review terms (Introduction, A Section, B Section, Interlude and Coda)
- Read and perform rhythm patterns *(ta, ta, ta, ta) (ti-ti, ti-ti, ti-ti, ta) (ta, ta, ti-ti, ti-ti)*
- Discuss the importance of exercise and good health

This lesson addresses National Standards for Arts Education, Music Grades K-4: 1b, 1e, 2a, 2d, 2f, 5a, 6a, 6c.

MATERIALS

- CD track 18 (with vocals); track 36 (accompaniment)
- CD player
- Visuals of following stick notation: *(ta, ta, ta, ta) (ti-ti, ti-ti, ti-ti, ta) (ta, ta, ti-ti, ti-ti)*
- Visuals with terms Introduction, Interlude, Coda and A Section, B Section

START

1. As the children assemble, play the accompaniment track and have children follow as you tap, changing placement every four beats (pat head, tap knees, pound fists, alternate pats, etc.)
2. When the song ends, have the kids stand up, and continue to follow your lead. Play the singing version and start the actions described in the song.
3. Play the A Section of the song again, pointing to the prepared visuals at the appropriate times, as the class listens and does the following.

- For the quarter note patterns *(ta, ta, ta, ta)*, patschen (pat the lap). For the eighth note patterns and one quarter note *(ti-ti, ti-ti, ti-ti ta)*, clap the eighths and pat the quarter.
4. Using the patschen/clapping movements, lead the children in performing the A Section of song. (NOTE: The melody skips from singing to accompaniment.)
5. Play B Section, performing patting and clapping as noted; add new visual for *ta, ta, ti-ti, ti-ti.*
6. Divide class into two sections, one for *ta's*, one for *ti-ti's*. Play the song again, and have the kids sing the rhythms as they perform them.

DEVELOP

1. Analyzing the song to help with memorization:
   - **Introduction** – Show the kids how to count multiple measure rests (1-2-3-4; 2-2-3-4; 3-2-3-4) This is how we should count sets for calisthenics.
   - **A Section** –draw simple icons for each phrase to help with memorization (shoe, smiley face, up-arrow/down-arrow, eyes).
   - **B Section** – memorize words as soon as possible, kids make up their own movements.
   - **A Section** – use the term **Repeat**; new icons (X for jumping jack; plus sign for "right way," forward-arrow/backward-arrow, thumbs up)
   - **B Section** – repeats
   - **Interlude** – bridges the first two verses to the Coda. Check to see if the kids recognize it from the introduction.
   - **Coda** – the ending. Start the movements smaller and the voice softer. Build to the BIG ENDING!
   - Map the whole song for the kids: **Introduction; A/B, A/B, Interlude, Coda.** Then lead the kids in singing the song, working for memorization of words and movements.
2. Lead a discussion of how important and fun exercising can be. Show the kids how to take their pulses, either at the wrist or neck.
3. Perform the song daily! Have children take their pulses before they sing and after.

WE CAN-CAN BE HEALTHY KIDS

Words by JOHN JACOBSON and JANET DAY
Music adapted from "The Galop" from
Offenbach's *Orpheus in the Underworld*

1st time: Children stretch and warm-up for exercise
2nd time: Children walk around room to take a breather

WHAT TIME IS IT, MR. CLOCK?

Lesson Plan by Judy Herrington and Connie Schmidt

LEARNING THROUGH ■
music

"Time flies when you are having fun!" Enjoy this lilting song with your class, adding instruments and sound effects. Classroom teachers will appreciate reinforcement of clock reading through your music class.

LESSON GOALS

- Sing in tune
- Maintain steady beat while singing
- Experience 6/8 meter
- Add mallet instrument accompaniments
- Practice mallet technique
- Recognize repeated patterns and sequence
- Experience anacrusis

This lesson addresses National Standards for Arts Education, Music Grades K-4: 1b, 1e, 2a, 2d, 5d, 6a, 6b.

MATERIALS

- CD track 19 (with vocals); track 37 (accompaniment)
- CD player
- Songsheet or visual of music for each student
- Percussion and barred instruments
- Charts of melodic phrases

START

1. You might find it helpful to give some preparatory experiences for the 6/8 meter. Echo-clapping rhythm patterns of 6/8 combinations is always fun and will often have students swaying and moving to the pulse. It can be helpful to have the beat flip from one side of the body to the other (i.e. "flip flop" the clap).

2. It is recommended that students have a visual of the music for reference. Create five charts, each with a melodic phrase from the song, but without the lyrics. Share with the students in mixed order. Sing the song and ask students to help you arrange the melody in the correct order. Teachable moments include:

- Melody has repeated sections
- Melody includes a scale sequence
- Form is AABBA
- Each phrase begins with a pick-up note, anacrusis

DEVELOP

1. Sing the entire song. If needed, echo phrase by phrase. You might find that your students do not need the echo and have discovered enough to try out the piece on their own. Praise them for their efforts in sight-reading.

2. Focus on accuracy of the anacrusis by having the students sing only the first two words of each phrase, the rest of the phrase is sung inside of the head. Practice that several times. Then divide into two groups; one group sings phrases 1 & 3; the other group sings phrases 2 & 4; and both groups sing the last phrase together.

3. During the rests that follow the singing, a student becomes the clock and demonstrates a position for the time. Glockenspiels may perform double octaves on the note C to indicate the clock's time. Students can then tell the time based on the number of quarter note "chimes."

Keep in mind the child that is the "clock hand" must think in reverse direction (mirror). Consider creating a large clock against the wall and have the teacher arrange the arms (add a mallet or rhythm stick in one hand for the long hand) of the student.

4. A possible barred instrument orchestration is available online in the Teachers' Corner Extension Activities section of the Music Express website. Log on to www.musicexpressmagazine.com, click on Teachers' Corner, then Extension Activities.

EXTENDED ACTIVITY

Children are often intrigued by the opportunity to study mechanical devices. Show a metronome to your class and describe its functions. Try setting the tempo for a very slow speed, and then sing, "What Time Is It, Mr. Clock?" with the metronome. Try a fast tempo, and then try the tempo as indicated.

WHAT TIME IS IT, MR. CLOCK?

Classroom prop needed: Child-size clock face drawn on wall or clock numbers taped to wall. Child creates time using arms. One hand is holding a rhythm stick to indicate the "long" hand.

Words and Music by JOHN JACOBSON and JANET DAY

4 measures introduction

Lilting tick-tock (♩. = 80)

What time is it, Mis-ter Clock? I hear you say tick and tock. So
stand up tall a-gainst the wall and move your hands, we'll un-der-stand the
time on the clock, tick tock.

Student comes forward to clock and uses arms to create a time.

Repeat as necessary

Class or selected student shouts out time created on clock.

Back to M. 11, repeat as needed

It's time to re-set the clock
(Last time) It's time for this song to stop!